M A R S
THE RED PLANET

ELIZABETH CARNEY

NATIONAL
GEOGRAPHIC
KiDS

WASHINGTON, D.C.

CONTENTS

HEY, NEIGHBOR!

Picture this: Pink skies. Orange sunsets.

Vast deserts and sprawling canyons. You can see these sites and more . . . on Mars!

This planet is one of Earth's nearest neighbors in the solar system. But it's still far away. It would take about six months to travel there in a spacecraft.

Throughout our history, Mars has seemed out of humans' reach. But that is changing. For 50 years, Mars-bound probes and robotic explorers have been beaming back exciting discoveries. Now missions to send people to Mars and back are being planned. The dream of humans traveling to Mars could soon be a reality.

In the meantime, this book will tell you everything you need to know about Mars. Plus, you'll see what missions could be like for brave explorers of the red planet. So you can decide:

Do you want to be among them?

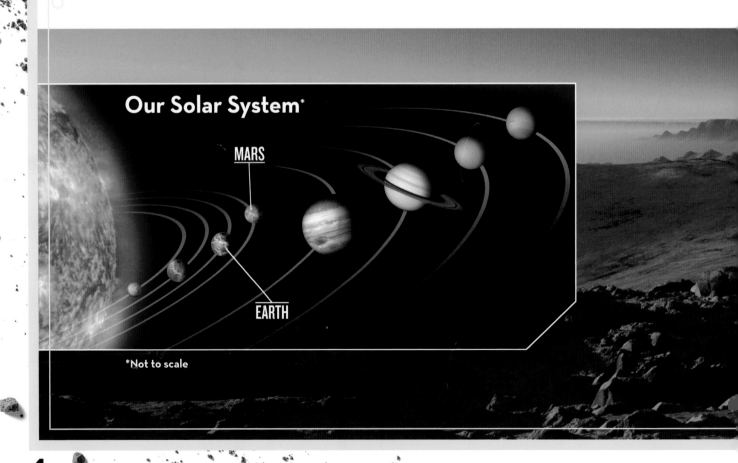

Our Solar System*

MARS

EARTH

*Not to scale

	EARTH	MARS
LENGTH OF DAY	24 HOURS	24 HOURS, 39 MINUTES
LENGTH OF YEAR	365 DAYS	687 DAYS
AVERAGE TEMP	59°F (15°C)	-81°F (-63°C)
DIAMETER	7,926 MILES (12,756 km)	4,222 MILES (6,795 km)
MOONS	ONE	TWO

Mars is the fourth planet from the sun.

It's about half the size of Earth. Only Mercury is smaller.

Mars has four seasons in the same order as we do on Earth: spring, summer, fall, and winter. But Mars takes twice as long to orbit the sun as Earth does. So the length of each Martian season is doubled, too. Imagine summer break on Mars. It would last six months!

Like Earth, Mars is a rocky planet. It has valleys and volcanoes, just like Earth does. In some ways, Mars is very similar to our planet. But there are also a lot of differences. That's part of what makes Mars so interesting.

THIS ART SHOWS AN ASTRONAUT AT THE MARINER VALLEYS ON MARS.

RED PLANET

Mars has fascinated sky-watchers for thousands of years. More than 2,000 years ago, ancient Romans noticed a small red glow when they gazed at the night sky. They named the planet Mars, after their god of war. The planet's color reminded them of blood. The name stuck. Today, the nickname for Mars is "the red planet."

The red planet's rosy color looks like rust. In a way, it is. The dusty soil on Mars contains iron. Iron is a metal and the main ingredient in rust. This makes Mars look like a ball of metal left out in the rain.

Future Mars explorers will find many features on the red planet that remind them of home. Mars has a solid surface with almost as much land area as Earth. Mars has a north and a south pole, where water is frozen all year round. (Sound familiar?) And just like on Earth, landforms such as valleys, canyons, and mountains stud Mars's surface.

MARS AS SEEN OVER MOUNT TAFTAN, IRAN

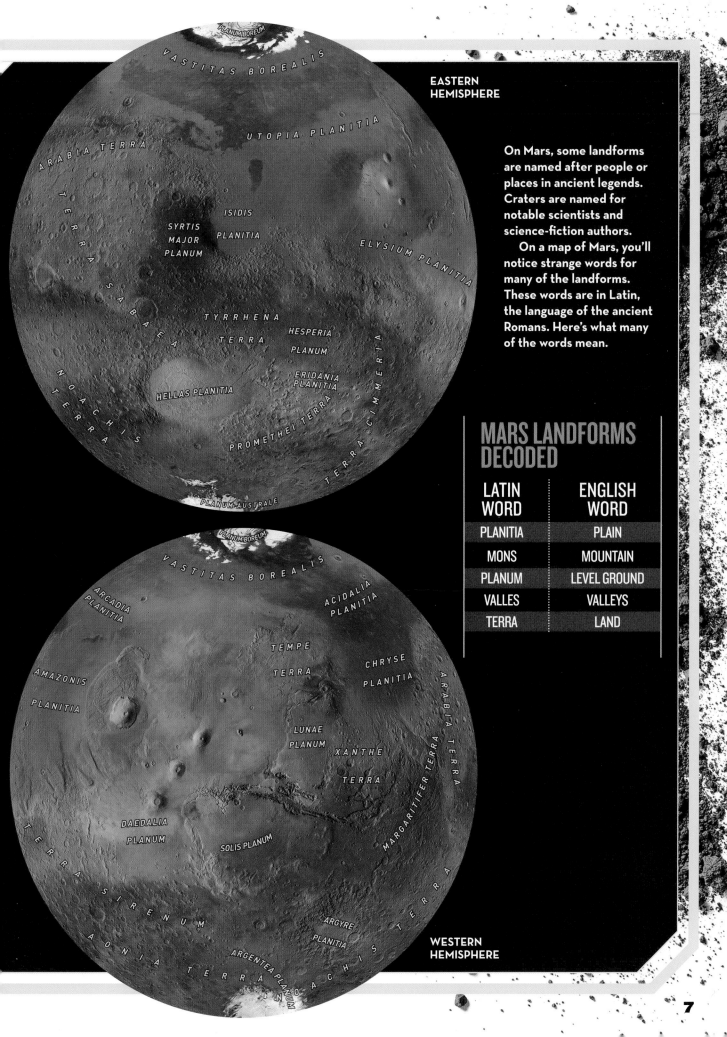

On Mars, some landforms are named after people or places in ancient legends. Craters are named for notable scientists and science-fiction authors.

On a map of Mars, you'll notice strange words for many of the landforms. These words are in Latin, the language of the ancient Romans. Here's what many of the words mean.

MARS LANDFORMS DECODED

LATIN WORD	ENGLISH WORD
PLANITIA	PLAIN
MONS	MOUNTAIN
PLANUM	LEVEL GROUND
VALLES	VALLEYS
TERRA	LAND

PLANUM BOREUM

VASTITAS BOREALIS

UTOPIA PLANITIA

ARABIA TERRA

TERRA SABAEA

ISIDIS

SYRTIS MAJOR PLANUM

PLANITIA

ELYSIUM PLANITIA

TYRRHENA TERRA

HESPERIA PLANUM

NOACHIS TERRA

ERIDANIA PLANITIA

HELLAS PLANITIA

TERRA CIMMERIA

PROMETHEI TERRA

PLANUM AUSTRALE

PLANUM BOREUM

VASTITAS BOREALIS

ARCADIA PLANITIA

ACIDALIA PLANITIA

TEMPE TERRA

CHRYSE PLANITIA

AMAZONIS PLANITIA

ARABIA TERRA

LUNAE PLANUM

XANTHE TERRA

DAEDALIA PLANUM

MARGARITIFER TERRA

SOLIS PLANUM

TERRA SIRENUM

ARGYRE PLANITIA

AONIA TERRA

ARGENTEA PLANUM

NOACHIS TERRA

COLD WORLD

Red-colored Mars looks blazing hot.

But it's actually freezing cold. It's farther from the warming sun than Earth is. Plus, its thin atmosphere isn't good at holding in heat. Earth's thick atmosphere holds in the sun's heat like a blanket. But on Mars, most of the heat bounces back into space.

Similar to Earth, temperatures on Mars vary wildly with the seasons. During the winter, lows can reach an incredibly cold -284°F (-176°C) in some locations. But during the height of a Mars summer, temperatures can reach a balmy 70°F (21°C) during the day.

Don't expect the T-shirt weather to last, however. Because of the wispy atmosphere on Mars, temperatures plunge at night no matter what the season. An average of -99°F (-73°C) is common after sunset.

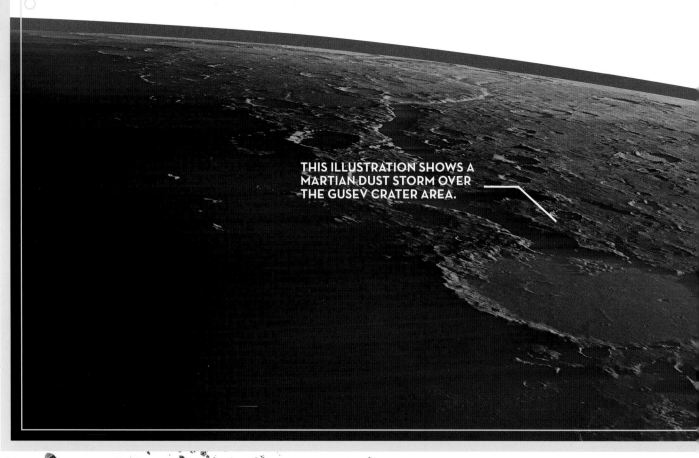

THIS ILLUSTRATION SHOWS A MARTIAN DUST STORM OVER THE GUSEV CRATER AREA.

AVERAGE TEMPERATURE ON EARTH: 59°F (15°C)

AVERAGE TEMPERATURE ON MARS: -81°F (-63°C)

100°
50°
0°
-50°
-100°

Extreme Conditions

A good winter coat won't be enough to keep you safe on Mars. Did you know that the air on Mars would be toxic for us? The atmosphere is made up mostly of carbon dioxide. That's the gas we breathe out. Earth's atmosphere is made up mostly of nitrogen and oxygen, the gas we need to live. Since there's no oxygen to breathe on Mars, visitors there will have to wear space suits that supply oxygen. The outfit you pack for Mars would literally mean life or death!

If that doesn't make you want to pass on a ticket to Mars, consider this: Planet-wide dust storms blanket Mars for months. In addition, tornadoes of dust called dust devils often swirl over the surface. They can reach heights of 3,000 feet (914 m).

Here's a bit of good news: Wind speeds max out at about 65 miles an hour (105 km/h). And since the atmosphere on Mars is so thin, wind speeds don't pack the punch of blustery gales on Earth.

A RESEARCHER TESTS A SPACE SUIT DURING A TRAINING SESSION.

10 COOL THINGS ABOUT MARS

OLYMPUS MONS ON MARS

MOUNT EVEREST ON EARTH

1

Mars is home to the tallest volcano in the solar system. This volcano, called Olympus Mons, is three times as high as Mount Everest!

2

Flakes of frozen carbon dioxide, or dry ice, fall as snow on Mars!

4

Mars, along with Mercury, has the lowest surface gravity in the solar system. If you weigh 100 pounds (45 kg) on Earth, you would weigh only 38 pounds (17 kg) on Mars!

3

The dust on Mars contains iron. That means it's magnetic. Mars explorers would be able to use magnetic brushes to pull the dust off their space suits!

5

Mars has a canyon that's more than five times as deep as the Grand Canyon. It would stretch from New York to San Francisco.

GRAND CANYON

6

Mars's oldest rocks show evidence that the red planet once had a strong magnetic field—like Earth does today. But billions of years ago, this magnetic field stopped. The reason why is a mystery.

7

The 1898 novel *War of the Worlds* by H. G. Wells was the first fictional story about a Martian invasion.

8

Experts predict that in the next 20 to 40 million years, the forces of gravity will tear apart Phobos, Mars's largest moon. Phobos will end up as a ring of debris around the red planet.

9

Ancient Chinese astronomers called Mars "the fire star."

10

On Mars, the sun appears about half the size it does on Earth. This is because of the shape of Mars's orbit and its distance from the sun.

MARTIAN LIFE?

Mars has long held a special place in people's imaginations. In books, television, and movies, Martians are often shown as little green men. And many famous movies feature superintelligent Martians with amazing technology. The idea that aliens live on Mars began more than 100 years ago.

In the late 1800s, some astronomers claimed to see channels on the surface of Mars through their telescopes. They believed that the channels were canals. They thought that Martians had built the canals to transport water to cities. The canals, it turns out, don't exist. But the idea that Mars might have advanced life-forms remained. Today, we know that's not the case.

MICROBES SEEN
THROUGH A
MICROSCOPE

POSTERS FROM TWO FAMOUS ALIEN FILMS SHOW WHAT SOME PEOPLE IMAGINED MARTIANS MIGHT BE LIKE.

JACK NICHOLSON · GLENN CLOSE · ANNETTE BENING · PIERCE BROSNAN · DANNY DeVITO

NICE PLANET. WE'LL TAKE IT!
MARS ATTACKS!

FryDay December 13

YOUR FAVORITE NEWSPAPER ADVENTURE HERO ON THE SCREEN AGAIN!
NEW WORLDS TO CONQUER
CHAPTER No. 1
OF THE New UNIVERSAL PICTURE
FLASH GORDON'S TRIP TO MARS
with LARRY Buster CRABBE as "FLASH GORDON"

It's fun to think about what an imaginary Martian might look like. Or what it would be like to live on Mars in the future. But scientists are most interested in knowing if life ever existed on Mars in the past. Many believe there is a strong chance it did. What would this life have looked like?

It probably would look like one of the microbes in the photo on page 12. It would be too small to be seen without a microscope. We know from studies on Earth that microbes can survive in extreme conditions. In fact, scientists collected bacteria from a lake in Antarctica and put them in Mars-like conditions. They survived!

If microbes exist on Mars, then real Martians are similar to creatures that are all around us here on Earth.

THIS ART SHOWS WHAT AN ARTIST THINKS A MARTIAN CITY MIGHT LOOK LIKE.

WATER!

Scientists have been searching for life on Mars for decades. But one key had always been missing—proof of liquid water on Mars. Liquid water is necessary to support life as we know it. Since liquid water hadn't been spotted on the red planet, scientists thought life couldn't exist there. In 2015, everything changed. Scientists announced evidence of flowing water on Mars!

Scientists already knew that water, locked up as ice, covers the north and south poles of Mars. They also knew that the red planet had rivers, lakes, and maybe even an ocean billions of years ago.

Then scientists spotted the water on photos beamed back from a spacecraft circling Mars. They saw dark streaks running down a mountainside. The streaks change with the Martian seasons. They grow longer in the summer. In the winter, they shrink and disappear.

Scientists studied the streaks with an instrument on the spacecraft. The result? The streaks are probably very salty water. The water runs down Mars's slopes when it's warmer and freezes in the cold.

LAYERS OF ICE ARE EXPOSED IN A CLIFF IN THE NORTH POLAR REGION OF MARS.

COMPUTER ARTWORK SHOWS WHAT RIVERS ON MARS MIGHT HAVE LOOKED LIKE 3.5 BILLION YEARS AGO.

Now you may be thinking, "I thought it was always freezing cold on Mars." It is! Even at the height of a Martian summer, average temperatures hover around -10°F (-23°C). But the water in these streaks is so salty, it has a lower freezing point than plain water. It's like the way salt keeps water from freezing on roads and sidewalks during winters on Earth.

Where is the water coming from? And is there life inside these salty streams? Scientists are still puzzling over these mysteries.

DARK STREAKS AT MARS'S HALE CRATER

NEXT STOP, MARS!

The best way to find out if life exists on Mars—or if it ever did—is to pay the planet a visit. For the past 50 years, scientists have been doing just that. Except that spacecraft, not humans, have been making the trip.

Early spacecraft were made of the best technology available at the time. Still, they were simple compared to what we send to Mars today. Mariner 4 returned only 22 photographs of the surface of Mars.

Later spacecraft were like two vehicles in one. Viking 1 and Viking 2 had two

Check out some major milestones in Mars exploration in the timeline below.

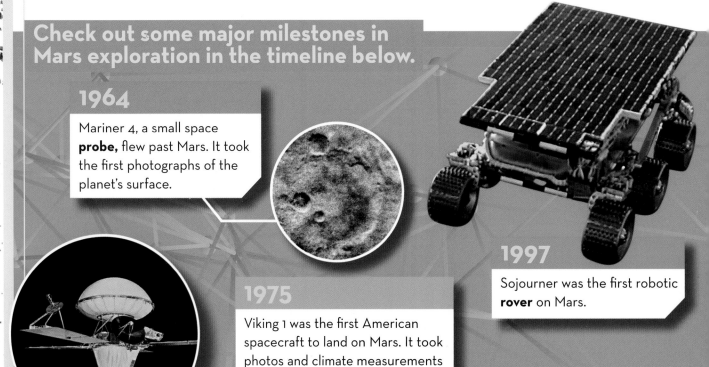

1964
Mariner 4, a small space **probe,** flew past Mars. It took the first photographs of the planet's surface.

1975
Viking 1 was the first American spacecraft to land on Mars. It took photos and climate measurements for seven years.

1997
Sojourner was the first robotic **rover** on Mars.

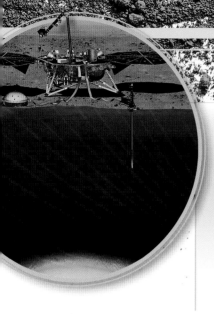

IN THE YEARS AHEAD

Scientists and engineers are preparing for the next robotic missions to Mars. A lander named InSight will soon journey to the red planet. Its job will be to study the interior of Mars—the part of the planet that's deep under the surface. This will give scientists clues about how the planet formed. A new rover is also under construction. It will look similar to Curiosity, but it will have more advanced instruments. The rover's arrival is planned for 2020.

parts—an orbiter and a lander. The lander touched down on Mars. The orbiter stayed in orbit around the planet.

Rovers are the most complicated Mars explorers yet. They roll over the surface taking pictures, soil samples, and measurements.

Four rovers have wheeled over the red planet. The first, Sojourner, was only the size of a microwave. It landed on Mars in 1997. Its mission was supposed to last 7 days. But Sojourner lasted 85 days. After traveling 330 feet (101 m), while snapping photos and doing experiments, it lost contact with mission control.

Over the past two decades, rovers have gotten bigger and much more powerful.

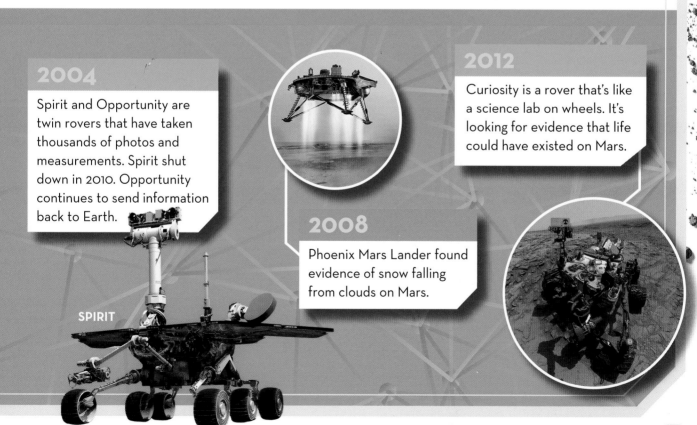

2004

Spirit and Opportunity are twin rovers that have taken thousands of photos and measurements. Spirit shut down in 2010. Opportunity continues to send information back to Earth.

SPIRIT

2008

Phoenix Mars Lander found evidence of snow falling from clouds on Mars.

2012

Curiosity is a rover that's like a science lab on wheels. It's looking for evidence that life could have existed on Mars.

CURIOSITY

Curiosity is the largest and most advanced rover sent to Mars.

It landed there in August 2012. The car-size rover is helping scientists study the red planet in more detail than ever before. Its mission was scheduled to last 23 months. But Curiosity outlasted that time frame and is still going strong. Its mission has been extended for now. It will likely continue for as long as the six-wheeled robot remains productive and in good condition.

Curiosity's job is to look for evidence of water in the rocks and soil on Mars. It's also looking for habitats where living things could have lived. To do this, Curiosity uses 17 high-tech cameras, a rock-zapping laser, and a nuclear-powered laboratory.

Since it arrived on Mars, Curiosity has been sending back important images and data. For example, it found carbon-based chemicals in rocks. Carbon is a building block of life. As a result, scientists have a better idea of where to look for ancient life on Mars during future missions.

Engineers on Earth control Curiosity's movements. After Curiosity landed on Mars, members of the control team switched to Martian time for three months. This helped them monitor the mission more easily.

The family of one flight director spent an entire summer on Mars time, too. After three weeks, their schedule was turned completely upside down!

Here's why: Mars rotates, or spins, more slowly on its axis than Earth does. This is why a Mars day, which is called a sol, lasts 39 minutes more than an Earth day. This difference might not seem like much, but it adds up. As the sols went by, Earth time and Mars time became very different. The family sometimes went to bed at noon and went bike riding at 3 a.m.!

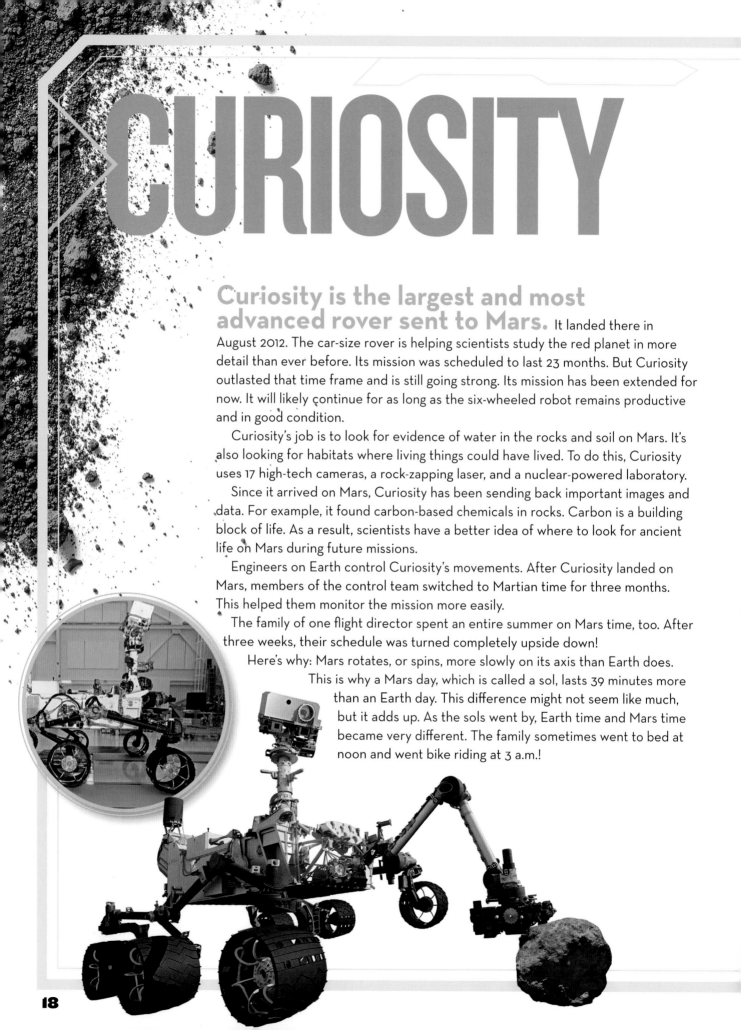

TO KEEP EARTH-BORN GERMS FROM HITCHING A RIDE TO MARS, TECHNICIANS AND ENGINEERS WEAR SPECIAL CLOTHING WHILE WORKING ON NASA'S CURIOSITY ROVER IN 2010.

PROTECTING ALIENS

After evidence of liquid water was found on Mars, some people wondered, "Why not send Curiosity to check it out?" It turns out that would actually be illegal!

Contamination (con-tam-uh-NAY-shun) is what would happen if microbes from Earth hitched a ride on a spacecraft or rover and started growing on another planet. If that happened, the Earthlings could harm life-forms in the alien environment. The Outer Space Treaty of 1967 forbids nations from putting life on other planets at risk in this way. The treaty requires nations to make sure any spacecraft, rovers, or human explorers avoid contaminating possible alien life.

Scientists can't be sure that Curiosity is completely microbe free, or sterile. Before the rover left Earth, it was cleaned with a blast of UV light. But Curiosity's equipment could only take so much. The high doses of light needed to prove that the rover was sterile would have damaged it.

During space travel, microbes hitching a ride on Curiosity probably went dormant, or inactive. Many probably died. But if any microbes survived, contact with water could wake them up. They might be able to grow and reproduce again. This could threaten any life that's already on Mars. So for now, scientists must investigate the water on Mars from afar.

CATHERINE CONLEY

Catherine Conley's job is to protect possible life on other planets from life on Earth. She's a planetary protection officer at NASA.

If a spot on Mars might be a place where Earth microbes can grow, scientists call the area a "special region." An area where the dark streaks of liquid salt water appear would be one of them. Special regions are off-limits to rovers.

But what if a rover stumbles on a special region by accident? Conley is studying how many microbes could remain on Curiosity after its time on Mars. As Curiosity zooms far from its landing spot, it might approach unexpected patches of water. Conley will advise mission scientists on what to do if that happens.

THE DARK STREAKS ON THESE HILLS MAY BE EVIDENCE OF WATER.

THIS SCAN OF A MARTIAN METEORITE SHOWS WHAT MAY BE A FOSSIL OF A BACTERIA-LIKE ORGANISM THAT LIVED BILLIONS OF YEARS AGO.

AN ARTIST'S DEPICTION OF CURIOSITY ON MARS

PEOPLE ON MARS

So far, scientists have sent only robots to Mars. But it may not be long before humans join them. Experts have different ideas on the best way to travel to Mars, but one thing is for sure: These types of missions to Mars would likely take years to complete.

The journey itself would take about six months. Once there, astronauts would likely have to set up areas to work, live, and grow their own food. To go outside, they would have to put on space suits. Talking to people at home would be difficult. Communication signals would take up to 20 minutes to reach Earth.

The United States plans to send astronauts to Mars by 2040. Space scientists are already planning what those brave explorers will wear! NASA recently showed off a new spacesuit for these missions, called the Z-2. It's designed for exploring the red planet. It's built to protect astronauts from the extreme conditions on Mars—freezing temperatures, solar radiation, and dust storms, to name a few.

The suit is also more lightweight and flexible than spacesuits of the past. That way, Mars explorers will be able to get to work on the planet's surface. They'll need suits that allow them to collect samples, construct habitats, and get in and out of rovers.

The Z-2 isn't mission-ready just yet. It's still being tested and tweaked here on Earth before it's ready for testing in space.

NASA'S Z-2 SUIT, A PROTOTYPE OF THE KIND OF SPACESUIT THAT MAY BE WORN ON MARS

THIS PROTOTYPE MAY BE SIMILAR TO THE KINDS OF HABITATS HUMANS COULD CONSTRUCT ON MARS.

DEEP SPACE HABITAT

HYGIENE MODULE

PREPPING FOR THE JOURNEY

Making sure that astronauts are Mars-ready will take a lot of equipment testing and training. So groups of scientists have created Mars-mission training grounds. They set up fake space stations so crews can practice surviving on the red planet.

Bases are often located in dry, empty areas that look like Mars, like the top of a Hawaiian volcano or a field in the Canadian arctic. Scientists hope to learn how to make a real-life Mars mission successful.

Current plans for Mars missions call for a crew of six astronauts. They'll each be trained for specific jobs, such as piloting a spacecraft or setting up electrical systems quickly and efficiently.

Mars mission plans include setting up temporary habitats (nicknamed "habs") and growing food on the red planet. But Mars explorers should pack all the food they'll need on the journey from Earth—plus some extra. They'll also need space suits, computers, tools, and life-support technology. This equipment, such as air and water recyclers, is essential for survival in space.

A MARS SIMULATION HABITAT ON MAUNA LOA IN HAWAII, U.S.A.

TWO SCIENTISTS PERFORM A TRAINING MISSION IN HANKSVILLE, UTAH, U.S.A.

TRAVELING TO MARS

Before you pack your bags to Mars, you should know how the journey could affect you.

Since Mars doesn't have supermarkets, astronauts will have to prepare and grow their own food. Scientists are studying what astronauts will eat when they're 150 million miles (241 million km) from Earth.

Any food brought from Earth will require at least a three-year shelf life. Mars travelers also need nutritious food so they don't get sick. A variety of food will help keep them from getting bored. Astronauts might be able to grow plants like strawberries and tomatoes in a greenhouse once they're on Mars.

Astronauts on the International Space Station are already perfecting space-farming techniques. On a recent mission, they harvested a crop of romaine lettuce that they grew entirely in space. The station's crew ate half of the harvest and sent the rest back to Earth to be studied. Such experiments make sure that deep-space travelers will have enough to eat during their Mars mission.

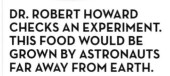

DR. ROBERT HOWARD CHECKS AN EXPERIMENT. THIS FOOD WOULD BE GROWN BY ASTRONAUTS FAR AWAY FROM EARTH.

PEPPERONI, PLEASE!

No pizza delivery on Mars? No problem! Astronauts on Mars may be able to "print" a pie with a 3-D printer. Scientists are working on a device that makes food with ingredients such as flavored powders, water, and oil at the push of a button.

Living in space can have some wild effects on the human body. Why? Our bodies are suited for life on Earth. We're used to having the force of gravity constantly tugging on our bones and muscles.

During space travel, the pull of Earth's gravity gets weaker the farther you get from the planet. Until a spacecraft reaches Mars and is under the pull of that planet's gravity, objects float in a state of weightlessness. Without gravity's strong pull, some body systems start to go haywire.

Muscles get weaker and bones can break easily. Fluid can build up at the top of the body, making the face puffy and the legs look shrunken. The fluid shift can also harm astronauts' vision.

Fortunately, exercise and a special diet can control some of these effects. On the International Space Station, astronauts exercise for two and a half hours a day. They bike on a stationary bike and run on a treadmill. They also "lift weights" using a special resistance machine.

ASTRONAUT SUNITA WILLIAMS IS TIED TO THE TREADMILL SO SHE WON'T FLOAT AWAY.

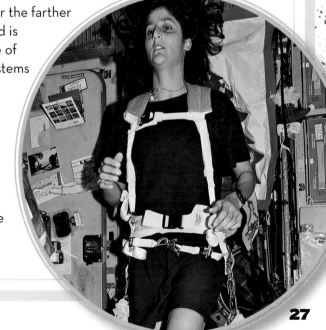

GREENING THE RED PLANET

YEAR ZERO

The project might begin with a series of missions to set up living quarters.

YEAR 100

Human-built factories could spew powerful greenhouse gases to boost Mars's atmosphere. The greenhouse gas buildup would begin to warm the frozen planet.

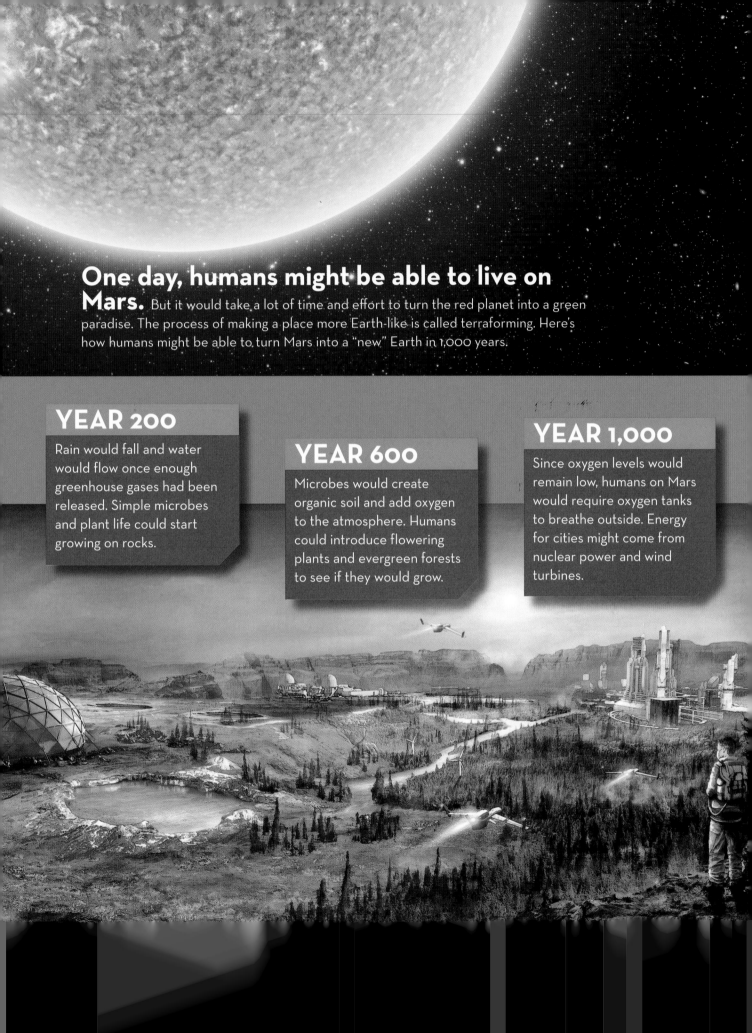

One day, humans might be able to live on Mars. But it would take a lot of time and effort to turn the red planet into a green paradise. The process of making a place more Earth-like is called terraforming. Here's how humans might be able to turn Mars into a "new" Earth in 1,000 years.

YEAR 200

Rain would fall and water would flow once enough greenhouse gases had been released. Simple microbes and plant life could start growing on rocks.

YEAR 600

Microbes would create organic soil and add oxygen to the atmosphere. Humans could introduce flowering plants and evergreen forests to see if they would grow.

YEAR 1,000

Since oxygen levels would remain low, humans on Mars would require oxygen tanks to breathe outside. Energy for cities might come from nuclear power and wind turbines.

INDEX

Boldface indicates illustrations.

PHOTO CREDITS

Front cover: (background), NASA/JPL-Caltech; (LO LE), Peter Bollinger; (LO CTR), Image Courtesy SpaceX; (LO RT), Henning Dalhoff/Science Source; **Spine:** David Aguilar; **Back cover:** (background), Stocktrek Images/Getty Images; (UP), JSC/NASA; (LO LE) JPL-Caltech/NASA; (LO RT), Peter Bollinger; **Interior:** throughout (red dirt), GalapagosPhoto/Shutterstock; 1, David Aguilar; 2-3, Stocktrek Images, Inc./Alamy; 4 (LO LE), NASA/Getty Images; 4-5, Detlev van Ravenswaay/Science Source; 5 (UP LE), David Aguilar; 5 (UP RT), David Aguilar; 6 (LO), Babak Tafreshi/National Geographic Creative; 8-9 (LO), Detlev van Ravenswaay/Science Source; 8-9 (background), Sergej Razvodovskij/Shutterstock; 9 (LO), Jim Olive/Polaris/Newscom; 10 (UP), David Aguilar; 10 (CTR), Dr. Mark Garlick; 10 (LO RT), Dimitri Vervitsiotis/Digital Vision/Getty Images; 11 (UP LE), Sumikophoto/Shutterstock; 11 (UP RT), MasPix /Alamy; 11 (LO LE), Babak Tafreshi/Science Source; 11 (LO RT), NASA/JPL-Caltech/Alamy; 12-13 (background), Angela Harburn/Shutterstock; 12 (LO), Steve Gschmeissner/SPL/Getty Images; 13 (UP LE), Warner Bros/Courtesy Everett Collection; 13 (UP RT), Everett Collection; 14 (LO LE), JPL-Caltech /Univ. of Arizona/NASA; 14-15 (UP), Sirocco/Shutterstock; 15 (UP), Kees Veenenbos/Science Source; 16 (LO LE), NASA; 16 (LO CTR), NASA; 16 (LO RT), JPL/Caltech/NASA; 17 (LO LE), JPL/Cornell University, Maas Digital LLC/NASA; 17 (LO CTR), JPL/NASA; 17 (LO RT), JPL-Caltech/NASA; 18 (CTR LE), Science Source; 18 (LO RT), Detlev van Ravenswaay/Science Source; 19, JPL-Caltech/NASA; 20-21, Henning Dalhoff/Science Source; 20 (LO LE), W. Hrybyk/NASA; 21 (UP LE), NASA/Science Source; 21 (UP RT), Science Source; 22, NASA; 23, Peter Bollinger; 23 (UP), NASA; 24, Andrzej Stewart; 25, Ruaridh Stewart/zumapress.com; 25 (inset), Red Huber/MCT/zumapress.com; 26 (LO LE), Robyn Beck/AFP/Getty Images; 26 (LO LE), Rex Features /AP Images; 26 (LO CTR), Rex Features/AP Images; 26 (LO RT), Rex Features/AP Images; 27 (LO), NASNA/UPI/Newscom; 27 (UP), Peter Bollinger; 28-29 (LO), Stephan Morrel/National Geographic Creative; 28-29 (UP), Aphelleon/Shutterstock; 30-31 (background), Stocktrek Images/Getty Images; 32 (background), Stocktrek Images/Getty Images; 32 (UP), David Aguilar

MORE RESOURCES

Want to know more about the red planet and outer space?
Check out these other out-of-this-world books!

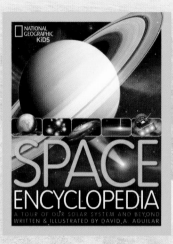

And for adults:

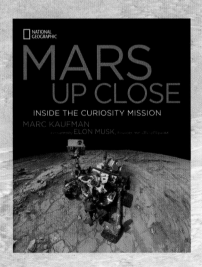

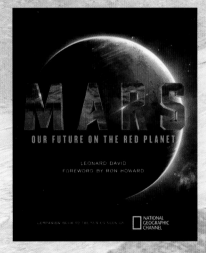

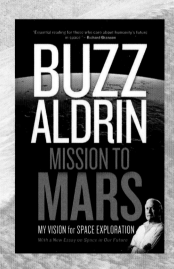

For every stargazer who has been inspired and humbled by the cosmos. —E.C.

CREDITS

Since 1888, the National Geographic Society has funded more than 12,000 research, exploration, and preservation projects around the world. The Society receives funds from National Geographic Partners LLC, funded in part by your purchase. A portion of the proceeds from this book supports this vital work. To learn more, visit www.natgeo.com/info.

NATIONAL GEOGRAPHIC and Yellow Border Design are trademarks of the National Geographic Society, used under license.

For more information, visit nationalgeographic.com, call 1-800-647-5463, or write to the following address:
National Geographic Partners
1145 17th Street N.W.
Washington, D.C. 20036-4688 U.S.A.

Visit us online at nationalgeographic.com/books

For librarians and teachers: ngchildrensbooks.org

More for kids from National Geographic:
kids.nationalgeographic.com

For information about special discounts for bulk purchases, please contact National Geographic Books Special Sales:
ngspecsales@ngs.org

For rights or permissions inquiries, please contact National Geographic Books Subsidiary Rights: ngbookrights@ngs.org

Library of Congress Cataloging-in-Publication Data

Names: Carney, Elizabeth, 1981- author. | National Geographic Society (U.S.)
Title: Mars : the red planet / by Elizabeth Carney.
Description: Washington, DC : National Geographic Kids, [2016] | Audience:
    Ages 6-9. | Includes index.
Identifiers: LCCN 2016027900 | ISBN 9781426327544 (pbk. : alk. paper) |
    ISBN 9781426327551 (library binding : alk. paper)
Subjects: LCSH: Mars (Planet)--Juvenile literature.
Classification: LCC QB641 .C37 2016 | DDC 523.43--dc23
LC record available at https://lccn.loc.gov/2016027900

Designed by Eva Absher-Schantz

Printed in the United States of America
16/WOR/1

The publisher gratefully acknowledges the expert review of this book by Dr. Kirsten Siebach of the California Institute of Technology and thanks the book team: Kathryn Williams, Shelby Alinsky, Eva Absher-Schantz, Hillary Leo, Lori Epstein, Alix Inchausti, and Anne LeongSon.